Phonics Reading 3

WorldCom Edu

Contents

Matt the Mole

PR3-01
MP3

Matt the mole digs many holes.

He digs in day or night.

He digs around poles.

He digs left and right.

He digs all the way to Rome.

He digs so far he can't find home.

He digs more and finds a bone.

He digs to find a phone.

Vocabulary

mole

bone

pole

phone

More words   Find the words.

1 hole

2 dig

3 Rome

4 left

t	u	e	d	d
f	e	l	g	x
e	m	o	i	b
l	o	h	d	i
r	R	v	t	c

Choose   Write the correct letters.

a

b

c

d

bone 

mole 

pole 

phone 

 Write the missing letters.

_____ole

_____ome

_____one

_____ole

 Choose the correct one.

All day he _________s and _________s.

a. jig   b. wig   c. dig

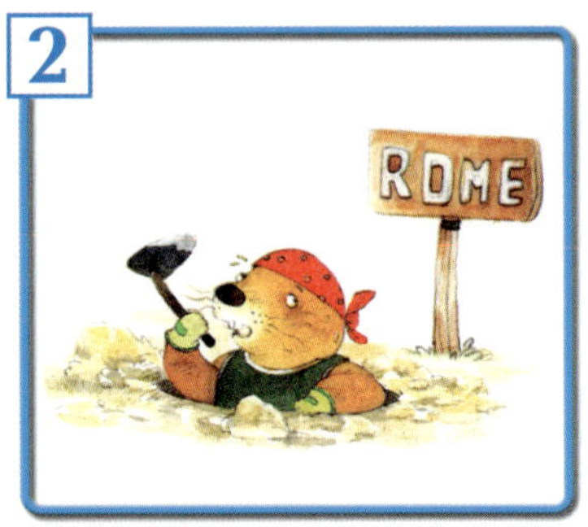

He digs all the way to _________.

a. Rome   b. Some   c. Come

Comprehension **Read and choose the answers.**

1 This story is about Matt the mole / pole .

2 Matt the mole digs many holes / poles .

3 He digs up and down / left and right .

Listen and Write  **Listen and write the correct words.**

pole	phone	home	Rome

1 He digs around __________ s.

2 He digs all the way to __________ .

3 He digs so far he can't find __________ .

4 He digs to find a __________ .

PR3-02
MP3

The monkey is on the p*ole*.

He hits the bell with a c*one*.

The lion hits it with a b*one*.

And he gets the same t*one*.

The m*ole* listens to the bell.

But he swings his bar wrong.

Now the duck sees stars.

And he has to go h*ome*.

Vocabulary

home

bell

tone

cone

More words Connect the words to the right pictures.
Then write the words.

1 bar   •   • 

2 listen   •   •

3 duck   •   •

4 swing   •   •

Unscramble Unscramble the words.

 1

 2

 3

 4

1 o n t e ➡

2 o h e m ➡

3 e l b l ➡

4 e c n o ➡

    Write the words that rhyme.

> mole   bone   tone   pole

1   -one   __________   __________

2   -ole   __________   __________

Choose   **Check ✔ the correct sentences.**

1

Now I see bells. ☐

Now I see stars. ☐

2

He hits the bell with a bar. ☐

He hits the bell with a bone. ☐

1 This story is about a bell / star .

2 But he swings / listens his bar wrong.

3 He hits the bell with a tone / cone .

Listen and Write  Listen and write the correct words.

home	bone	pole	tone

1 And he gets the same ___________.

2 And he has to go ___________.

3 The lion hits it with a ___________.

4 The monkey is on the ___________.

Unit 3 What are They Doing?

Ben and Bob play catch.

Susan reads by a rose.

Pete kicks a ball.

Jim blows his nose.

Josh jumps rope,

with a water hose.

He needs dry clothes.

And so does the Pope.

Vocabulary

rope

rose

hose

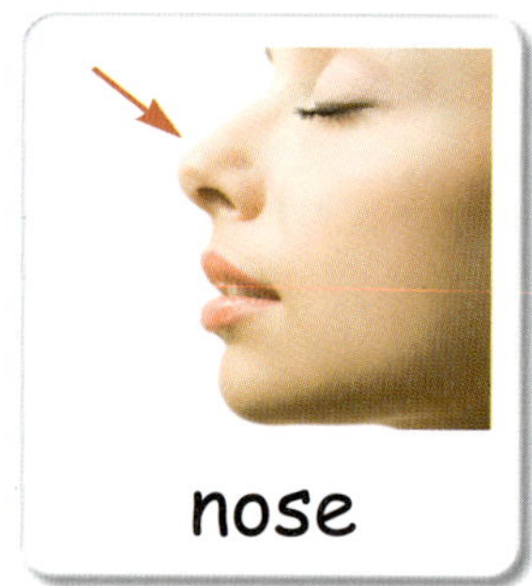

nose

More words Write the words.

1  pope

2  clothes

3  kick

4  blow

Complete Complete the words.

1 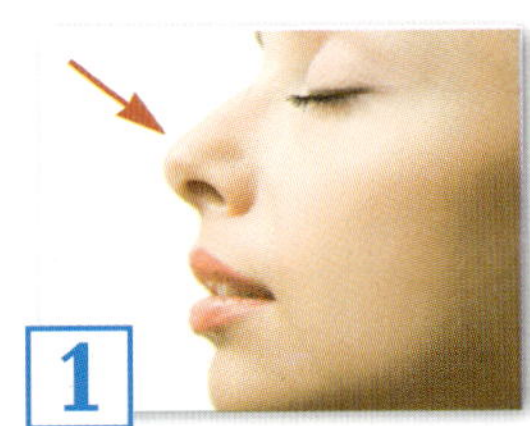 __ o __ e

2  r _____ e

3  r __ s __

4  h __ s __

  Choose the pictures rhyming with the words.

1 rose

2 nose

3 Pope

4 hose

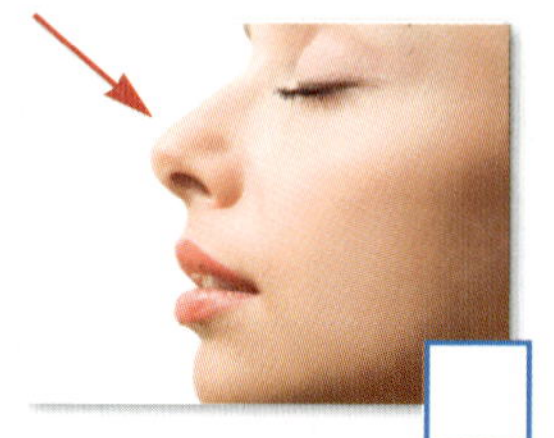 

True or False **Check ✓ True or False.**

1

Jim blows his nose.

T ☐ F ☐

2

I kick a ball.

T ☐ F ☐

Comprehension Read and choose the answers.

1 This story is about what they are doing / eating .

2 Jim blows his hose / nose .

3 And so does the Pope / rope .

Listen and Write  Listen and write the correct words.

rope	rose	catch	clothes

1 Susan reads by a ____________.

2 He needs dry ____________.

3 Josh jumps ____________, with a water hose.

4 Ben and Bob play ____________.

Review Unit 1~3

Check ✓ the right words and write.

1 
left ☐
bar ☐
kick ☐

2 
dig ☐
phone ☐
listen ☐

3 
swing ☐
duck ☐
blow ☐

4  
bone ☐
tone ☐
clothes ☐

Complete the crossword puzzles.

mole ➡

bone ⬇

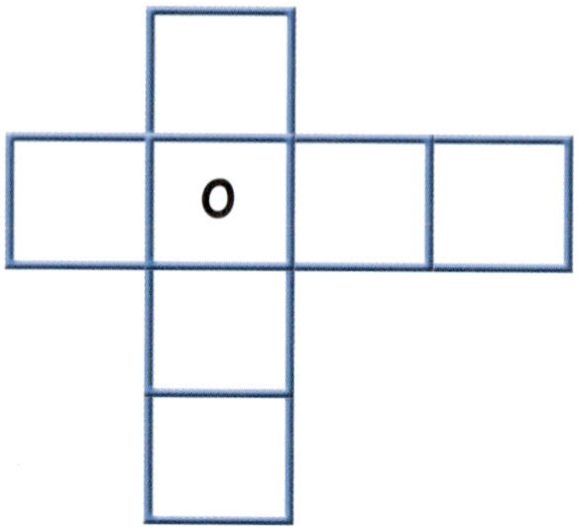

rose ➡

rope ⬇

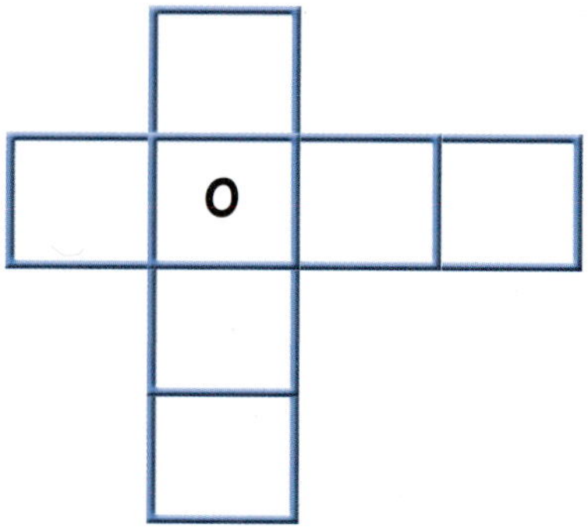

o

o

Check ✔ the correct letters.

1 

ose ☐
ole ☐

2 

ole ☐
ome ☐

3 

one ☐
ome ☐

4 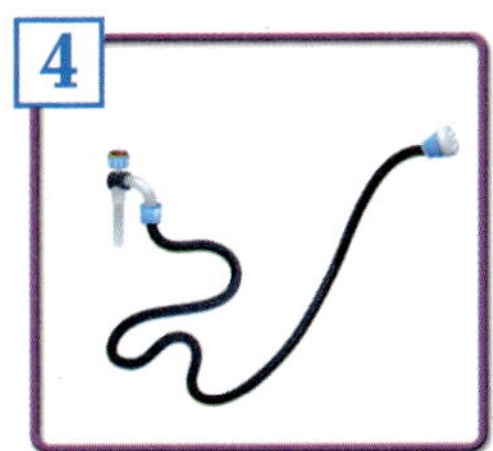

ope ☐
ose ☐

Circle the correct pieces and write.

1 

h
ome
ose
ole

2 

c
ome
ope
one

3 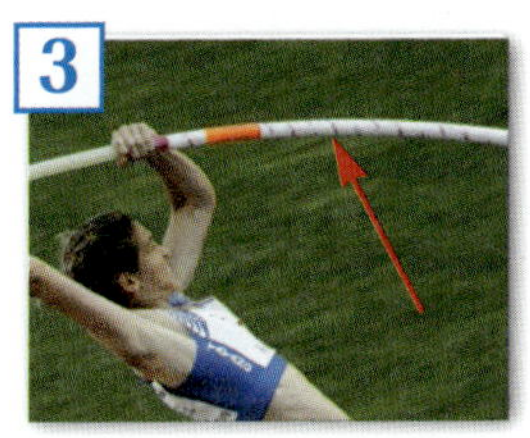

p
ote
one
ole

4 

h
ole
ome
ope

Molly the mule loves to sing.

She sings all day long.

She sings a tune on the dune.

It is a happy song.

But it's hard to sing in June.

The sun is just too hot.

Molly sits on an ice cube.

She drinks water from a pot.

Vocabulary

mule

sing

dune

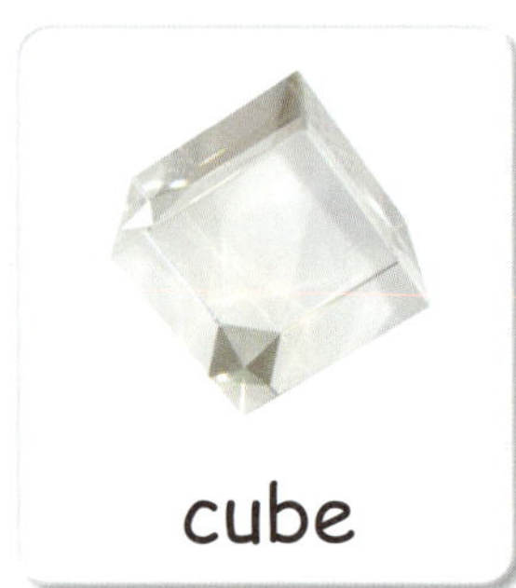

cube

More words — Find the words.

1. June

2. pot

3. tune

4. drink

d	t	t	u	z
n	r	u	o	a
t	t	i	n	p
n	n	e	n	e
e	n	u	J	k

Choose — Write the correct letters.

a

b

c

d

cube    dune 

sing    mule 

  Write the missing letters.

 _____une

 _____ube

 _____ule

 _____une

True or False Check ✔ True or False.

Molly the mule loves to sing.

T ☐ F ☐

Molly sits on the dune.

T ☐ F ☐

Comprehension **Read and choose the answers.**

1 This story is about Molly the [rule / mule].

2 Molly the mule loves to [sing / sit].

3 She sings a tune on the [June / dune].

Listen and Write  **Listen and write the correct words.**

| June | cube | water | sing |

1 But it's hard to sing in ___________.

2 Molly sits on an ice ___________.

3 She ___________s all day long.

4 She drinks ___________ from a pot.

Unit 5 Summer

Today is very hot.

It's the first day of June.

Our big ice cube melts.

Our plum is now a prune.

It's too hot on this dune.

Let's walk to the sea.

We can walk and sing a tune.

That's okay with me!

Vocabulary

prune

melt

plum

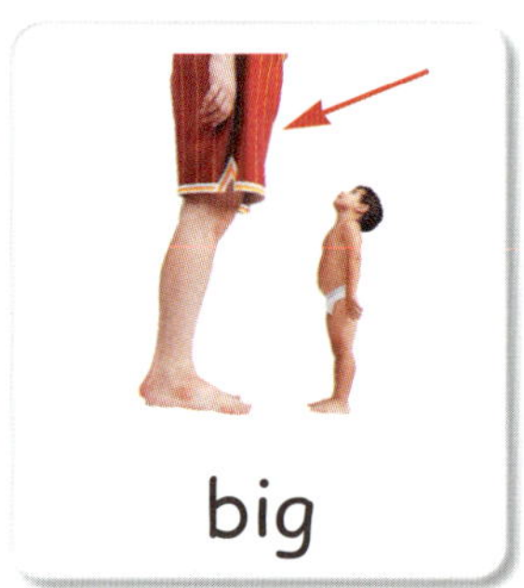

big

More words Connect the words to the right pictures.
Then write the words.

1 walk •

2 tune •

3 hot •

4 ice cube •

Unscramble Unscramble the words.

   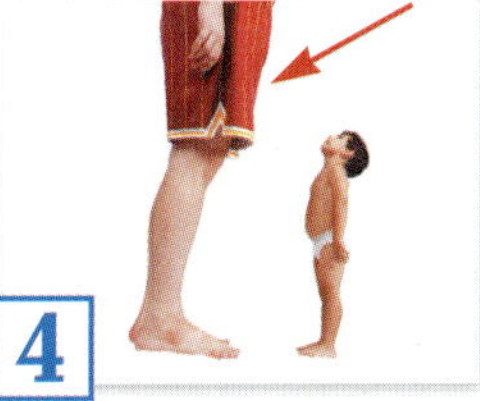

1 t m e l →

2 u l p m →

3 u p n r e →

4 i g b →

   Choose the pictures rhyming with the words.

1 June

2 tube

3 tune

4 June

True or False   **Check ✓ True or False.**

1

A big ice tube melts.

T ☐   F ☐

2

We can walk and sing a tune.

T ☐   F ☐

1 This story is about today's weather / tune .

2 It's the first day of June / dune .

3 Today is very cold / hot .

 **Listen and Write** Listen and write the correct words.

tune	cube	dune	prune

1 We can walk and sing a __________ .

2 Our plum is now a __________ .

3 It's too hot on this __________ .

4 Our big ice __________ melts.

Unit 6 — Let's Jump Rope

Three cute short mice,

look for rope or string.

But one mouse brings back,

a fuse with TNT.

The other two mice,

want to jump and scream.

But they are mute.

They can't say a thing!

Vocabulary

mute

string

cute

fuse

More words — Write the words.

1  scream

2  short

3  rope

4  jump

Complete — Complete the words.

1  ___u___e

2  c___t___

3 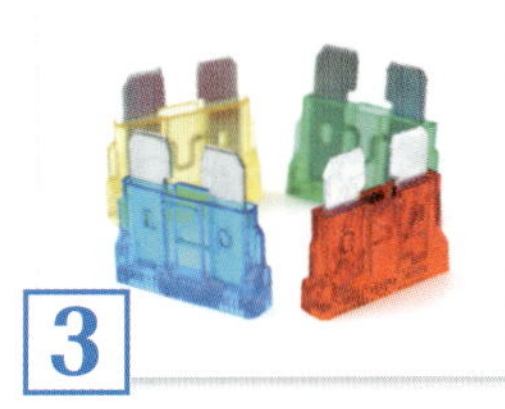 f______e

4 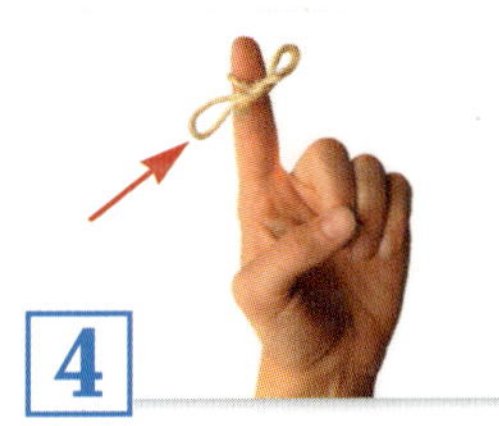 ___t___ing

  Write the words that rhyme.

fuse	cute	mute

1 -use ______________

2 -ute ______________   ______________

  Check ✔ the correct sentences.

The string is too short. ☐

The string is too long. ☐

One mouse brings a house. ☐

One mouse brings a fuse. ☐

1   This story is about three ⎯short / long⎯ mice.

2   Three mice look for ⎯rope or string / a fuse with TNT⎯ .

3   They are three ⎯mute / cute⎯ short mice.

Listen and Write    **Listen and write the correct words.**

say	fuse	mute	scream

1   But they are ____________.

2   The other two mice want to jump and ____________.

3   They can't ____________ a thing.

4   A ____________ with TNT.

No School for Me

PR3-07
MP3

I'm so sick today.

I can't get out of bed.

My nose runs and I can't smell.

There's a pain in my head.

I can't play my flute.

My clock says that it's three.

I don't think colds are cute.

Is there no cure for me?

Vocabulary

flute

cure

cold

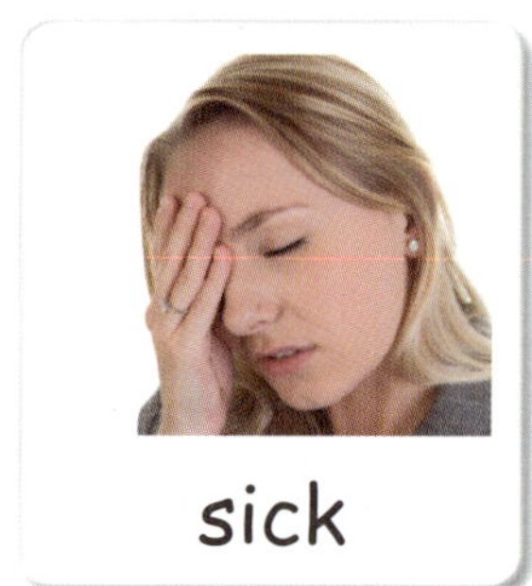

sick

More words Find the words.

1

clock

k	p	q	s	x
c	a	l	m	h
o	i	d	e	l
l	n	e	l	d
c	b	b	l	a

2

bed

3

pain

4
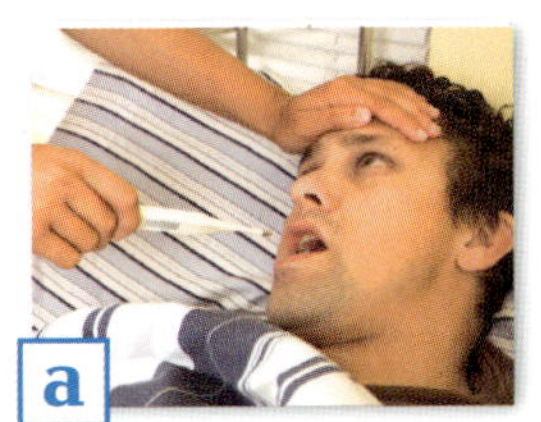
smell

Choose Write the correct letters.

a

b

c
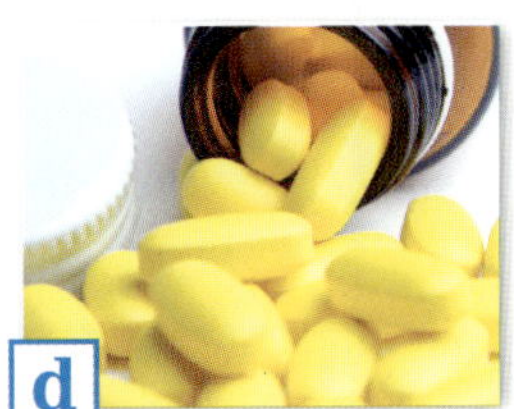

d

flute

cold

sick

cure

  Write the words that rhyme.

cure	cute

1 -ure __________

2 -ute __________

Complete **Choose the correct one.**

1 I can play my ________.

a. flute   **b.** piano   **c.** violin

2 I can't get out of ________.

a. boat   **b.** bed   **c.** head

  Read and choose the answers.

1 This story is about a a. cold b. cure .

2 I am so a. happy b. sick today.

3 Is there no a. cure b. clock for me?

   **Listen and write the correct words.**

| flute | cute | three | pain |

1 I can't play my ___________ .

2 My clock says that it's ___________ .

3 There's a ___________ in my head.

4 I don't think colds are ___________ .

Check ✓ the right words and write.

1 

drink ☐
plum ☐
kick ☐

2 

melt ☐
hot ☐
smell ☐

3 

short ☐
dune ☐
jump ☐

4 

pain ☐
clock ☐
prune ☐

Complete the crossword puzzles.

mule ➡

dune ⬇

fuse ➡

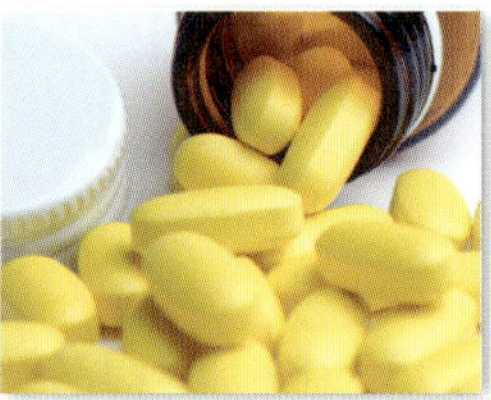

cure ⬇

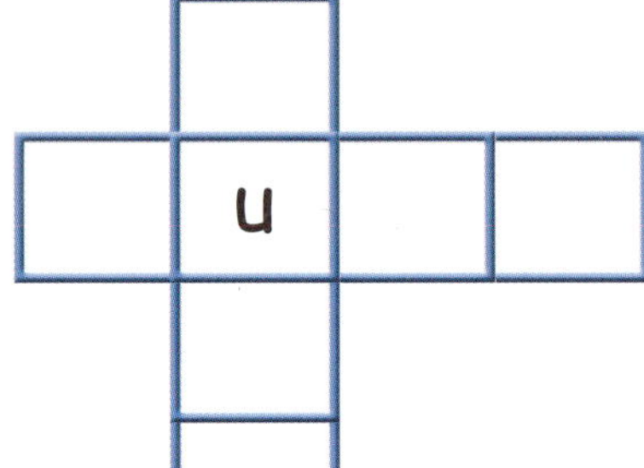

Check ✔ the correct letters.

1  ube ☐
ure ☐

2  ube ☐
ute ☐

3  ure ☐
une ☐

4  ule ☐
une ☐

Circle the correct pieces and write.

1  m ube / ute / use

2  c ube / use / ute

3  pr une / ule / ume

4  J ure / une / ule

Unit 8 — The Plant

Our class has a plant.

The plant is slim and small.

We want it to be big.

We want it to be tall.

But now it is too big.

It isn't slow to eat our books.

It eats the clock on the wall.

Please come and take a look!

Vocabulary

slim

class

plant

clock

More words — Find the words.

eat

book

wall

tall

k	w	k	i	b
l	o	a	x	b
o	y	o	l	m
t	a	e	b	l
t	a	l	l	h

Choose — Write the correct letters.

a

b

c

d

clock 

slim 

plant 

class 

Check ✔ the same double letter sound.

1 

play ☐
prune ☐

2 

glue ☐
clown ☐

3 

glad ☐
clean ☐

4 

slow ☐
plum ☐

Choose the correct one.

1 

Our class has a __________.

a. plum   b. plate   c. plant

2 

The plant eats the __________ on the wall.

a. class   b. clock   c. clothes

Comprehension Read and choose the answers.

1 This story is about the a. clock b. plant .

2 The plant is very a. cute b. small .

3 But now it's too a. slim b. big .

Listen and Write  Listen and write the correct words.

class	tall	slow	clock

1 It eats the ____________ on the wall.

2 It isn't ____________ to eat our books.

3 We want it to be ____________ .

4 Our ____________ has a plant.

PR3-09
MP3

In the winter snow,

I like to ride my sleigh.

I wear my winter gloves.
Because it's cold all day.

My sleigh is like a train,

that slides in the snow.

My sleigh is like a plane,

the faster that it goes.

Vocabulary

slide

plane

sleigh

gloves

More words   Write the words.

1 winter

2 ride

3 train

4 wear

Unscramble   Unscramble the words.

1

2

3

4

1 g v l o s e 

2 d e s i l

3 l a p e n

4 h i s g e l

Same letter — Check ✔ the same double letter sound.

1 

gl ☐
sl ☐
pl ☐

2 

pl ☐
gl ☐
sl ☐

3 

sl ☐
gl ☐
pl ☐

4

gl ☐
pl ☐
sl ☐

Choose — Check ✔ the correct sentences.

1 

☐ I like to wear gloves.

☐ I like to slide.

2 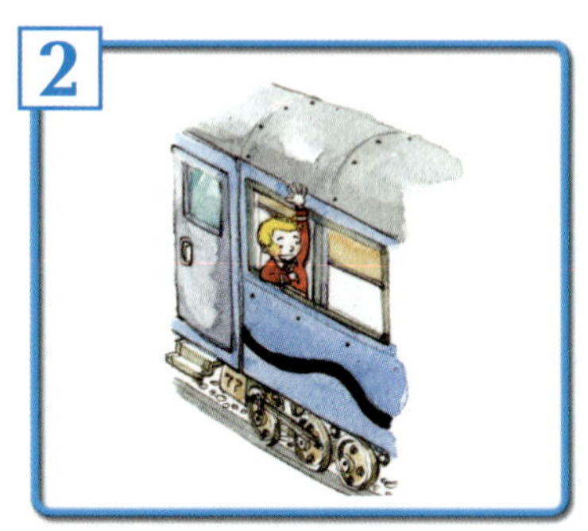

☐ I am on a train.

☐ I am on a plane.

Comprehension   Read and choose the answers.

1 This story is about snow / ride .

2 I like to ride my sleigh / plane .

3 My sleigh is slow / fast like a plane.

Listen and Write    Listen and write the correct words.

| winter | gloves | ride | sleigh |

1 I wear my winter ____________.

2 My ____________ is like a plane.

3 I like to ____________ my sleigh.

4 In the ____________ snow.

Review Unit 8~9

Check ✓ the right words and write.

1 

wall ☐
tall ☐
come ☐

____

2 

fast ☐
train ☐
winter ☐

____

3 

ride ☐
eat ☐
class ☐

____

4 

ride ☐
wear ☐
tall ☐

____

Complete the crossword puzzles.

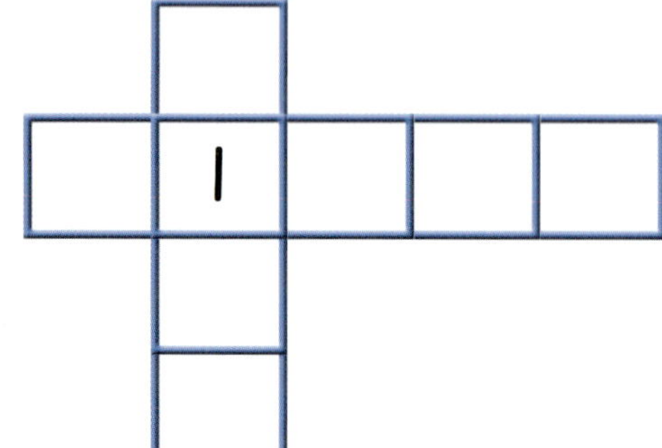

class ➡

slim ⬇

slide ➡

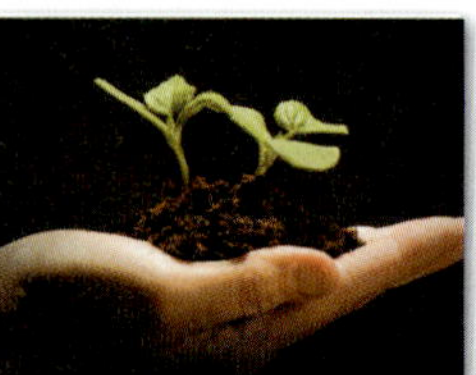

plant ⬇

Check ✓ the correct letters.

1 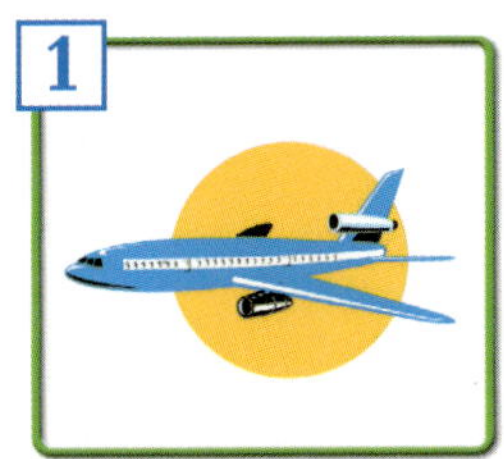
pl ☐
cl ☐

2
sl ☐
gl ☐

3 
sl ☐
cl ☐

4 
gl ☐
pl ☐

Circle the correct pieces and write.

1
sl
cl eigh
gl

2 
pl
gl ane
sl

3
sl
gl ide
pl

4 
pl
cl oves
gl

Our Wedding

The **bride** plays the **trumpet**.

The groom plays the **drum**.

The **frog** plays the piano.

Grandpa sings along.

Uncle dances in **front**.

Grandma dances wrong.

Everyone starts to dance

to the wedding song.

PR3-10
MP3

Vocabulary

bride

trumpet

drum

frog

More words   Write the words.

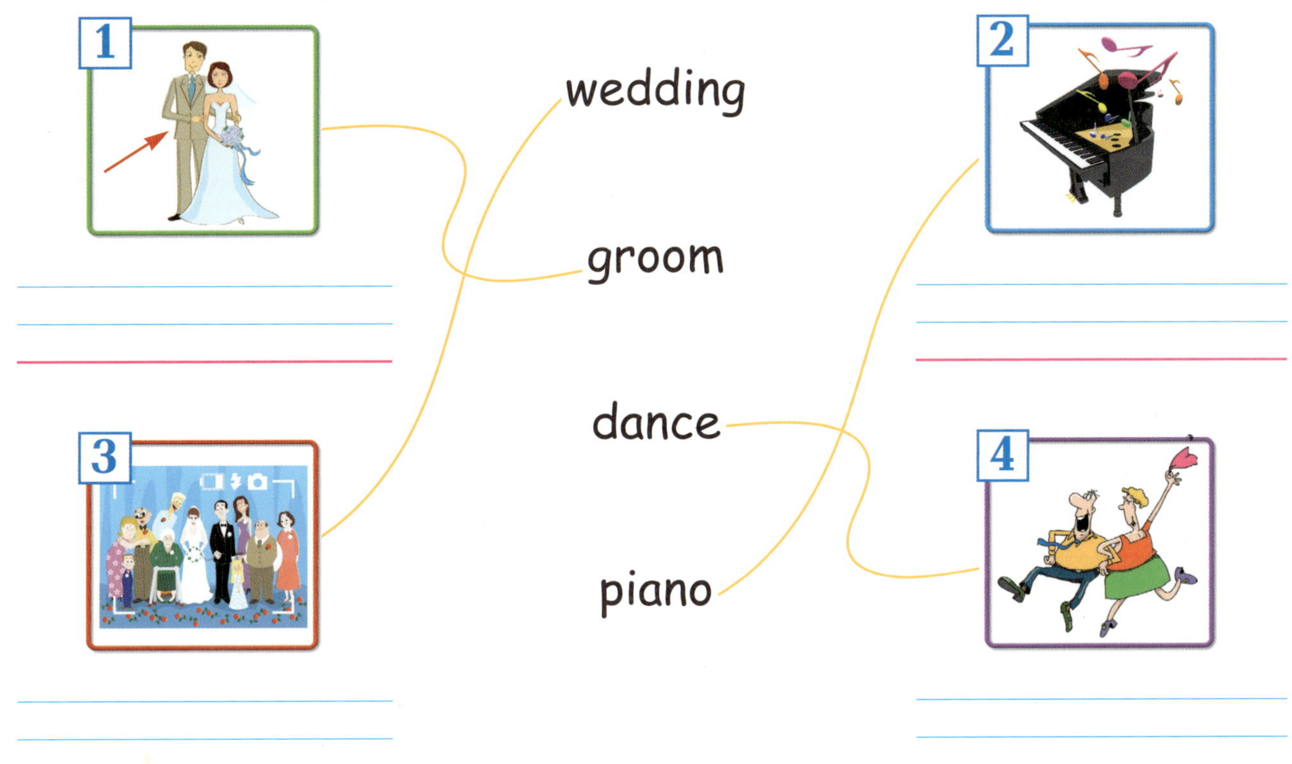

Complete   Complete the words.

d __ u __

__ r __ g

t __ um __ et

br __ d __

  Write the correct letters.

| dr | br | fr | tr |

1  **2**  **3**  **4** 

_____ide _____og _____um _____umpet

True or False Check ✔ True or False.

1 

Grandpa sings us a song.

T ☐ F ☐

2 

The frog plays the violin.

T ☐ F ☐

Comprehension   Read and choose the answers.

1   This story is about our [wedding / birthday] .

2   The groom plays the [drum / trumpet] .

3   [Grandma / Frog] plays the piano.

Listen and Write    Listen and write the correct words.

Grandpa	bride	dance	front

1   Uncle dances in __________ .

2   Grandma __________ s wrong.

3   The __________ plays the trumpet.

4   __________ sings along.

A Small Problem

My Dad drives a truck.

The truck has many things.

A picture frame and a train.

A dress and a gold ring.

He drives from the front.

And I begin to scream.

He didn't lock the tailgate.

And out come all the things.

Vocabulary

drive

dress

frame

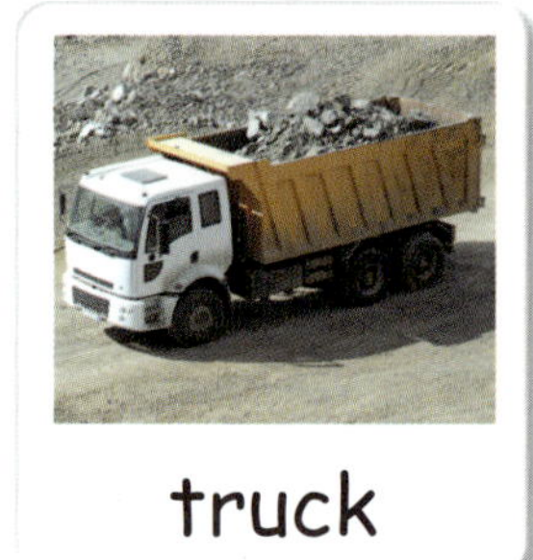

truck

More words — Find the words.

1

lock

2

train

3

ring

4

gold

t	n	u	p	m
r	d	l	o	g
a	j	q	d	z
i	k	c	o	l
n	r	i	n	g

Choose — Write the correct letters.

truck 

dress 

drive 

frame 

1 
brain ☐
train ☐

2 
drink ☐
blink ☐

3 
plum ☐
drum ☐

4 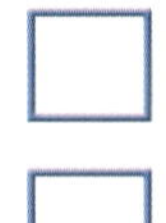
fresh ☐
flame ☐

Complete   Choose the correct one.

1 

My Dad drives a _______.

a. truck   b. train   c. trumpet

2 

A _______ falls from the truck.

a. toy   b. ring   c. shoe

1 This story is about a small question / problem .

2 My Dad drives a truck / train .

3 He didn't lock / open the tailgate.

Listen and Circle   Listen and circle the correct words.

1 A dress / drum and a gold ring.

2 The train / truck has many things.

3 A picture frame / friend and a train.

4 He dives / drives from the front.

Check ✓ the right words and write.

1 

frog ☐
piano ☐
groom ☐

2 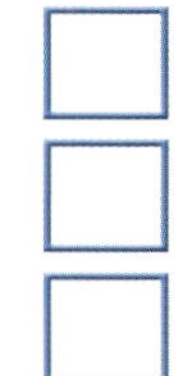

ring ☐
drum ☐
gold ☐

3 

dress ☐
bride ☐
groom ☐

4 

train ☐
trumpet ☐
drive ☐

Complete the crossword puzzles.

bride ➡

frog ⬇

dress ➡

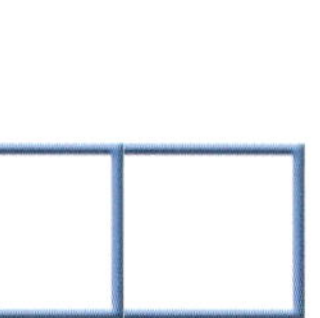

drum ⬇

r

r

Check ✓ the correct letters.

1 

tr ☐
dr ☐

2 

tr ☐
fr ☐

3 

br ☐
fr ☐

4 

dr ☐
tr ☐

Circle the correct pieces and write.

1 

fr
dr   ame
tr

____

2

br
dr   ive
fr

____

3 

fr
dr   umpet
tr

____

4

br
tr   ain
fr

____

Check ✔ the correct letters.

1  ome / one

2  ube / ule

3  cl / gl

4  fr / tr

Choose the correct pictures.

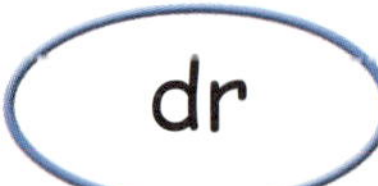

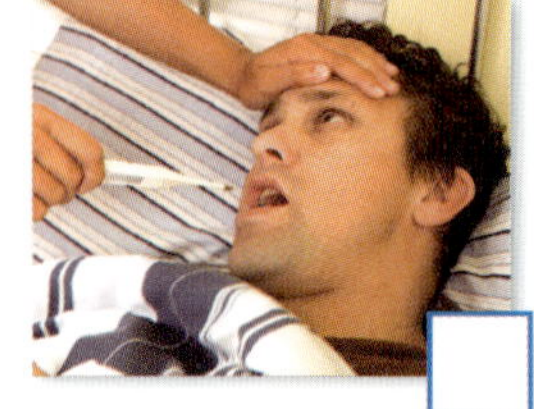 

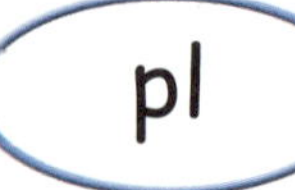

Check ✔ the words with the matching sound as the pictures.

1

clock ☐
wall ☐

2

pain ☐
pole ☐

3

drive ☐
ring ☐

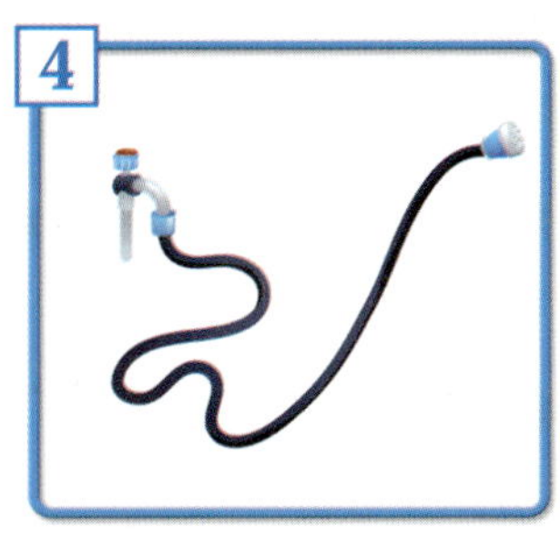

4

string ☐
nose ☐

5

smell ☐
slide ☐

6

blow ☐
cute ☐

7

frog ☐
tune ☐

8

mole ☐
plum ☐

Listen and write the missing word. Then put the correct letter matching to each sentence.

 a

 b

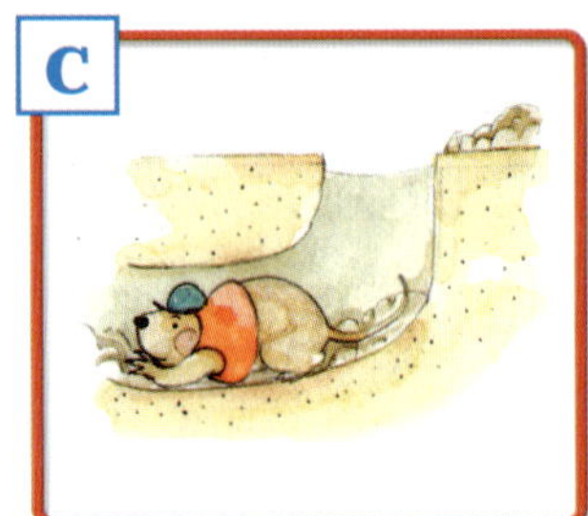 c

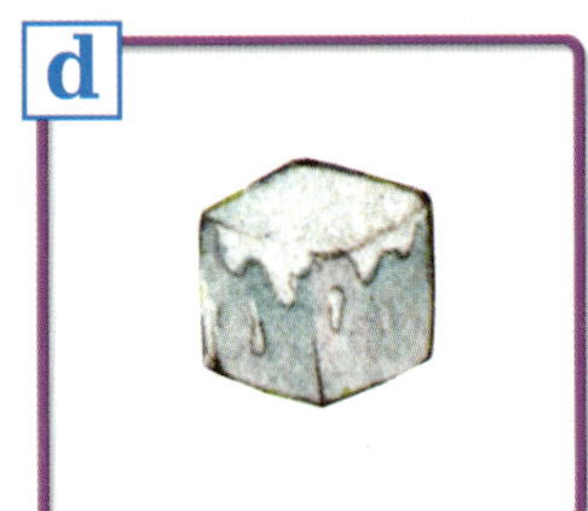 d

1 The mole _____________ s all day long. ☐

2 A big ice _____________ melts. ☐

3 They sing in _____________ . ☐

4 He _____________ s his nose. ☐

Look for Bones

We have bones in our hands.

We have bones in our toes.

There are bones in a mole.

There are no bones in a rose.

Are there bones in a mule?

I'm sure a mule has bones.

Are there bones in your home?

Maybe they are in your phone.

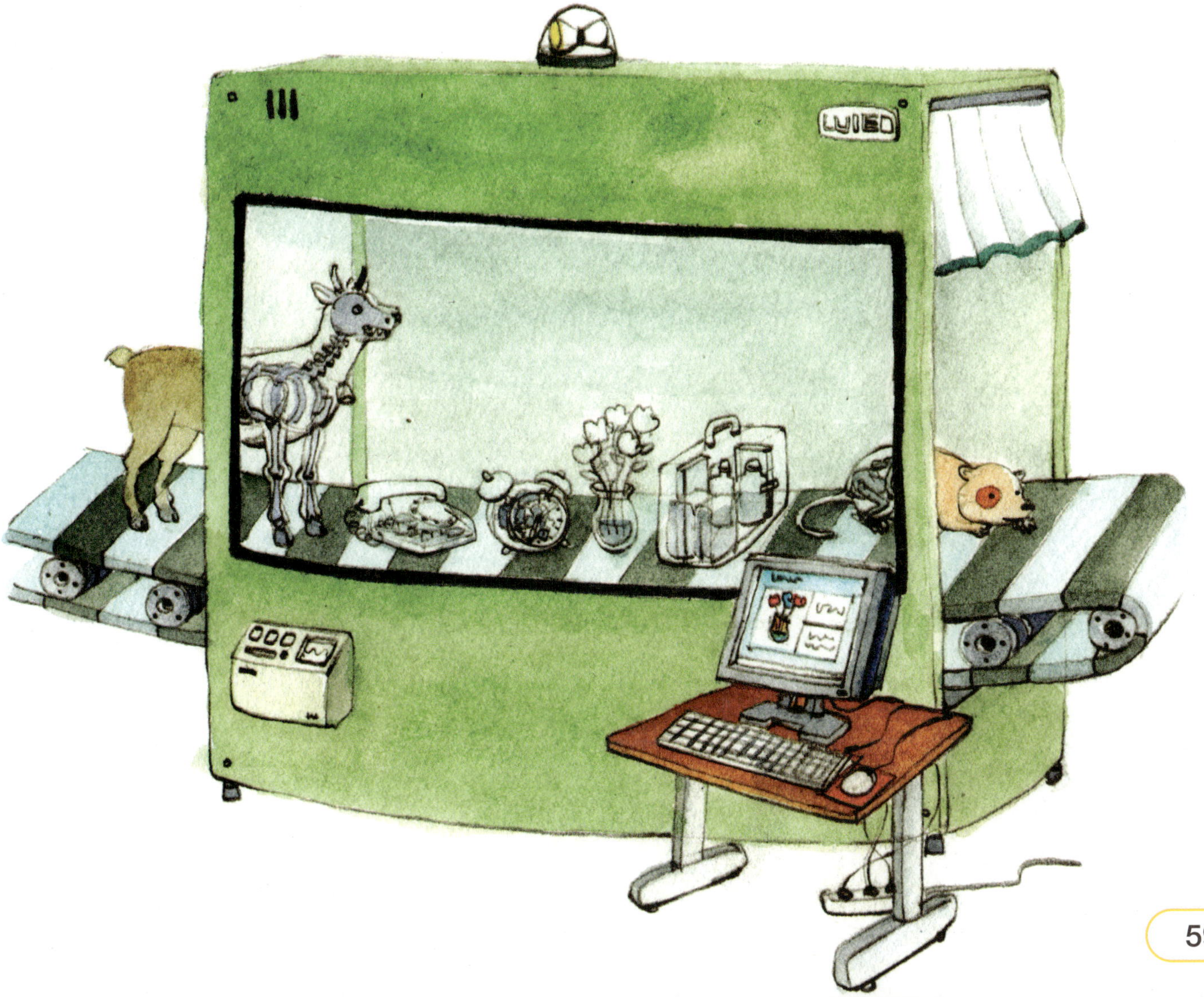

Photo Dictionary

Unit 1

- mole
- bone
- pole
- phone
- hole
- dig
- Rome
- left

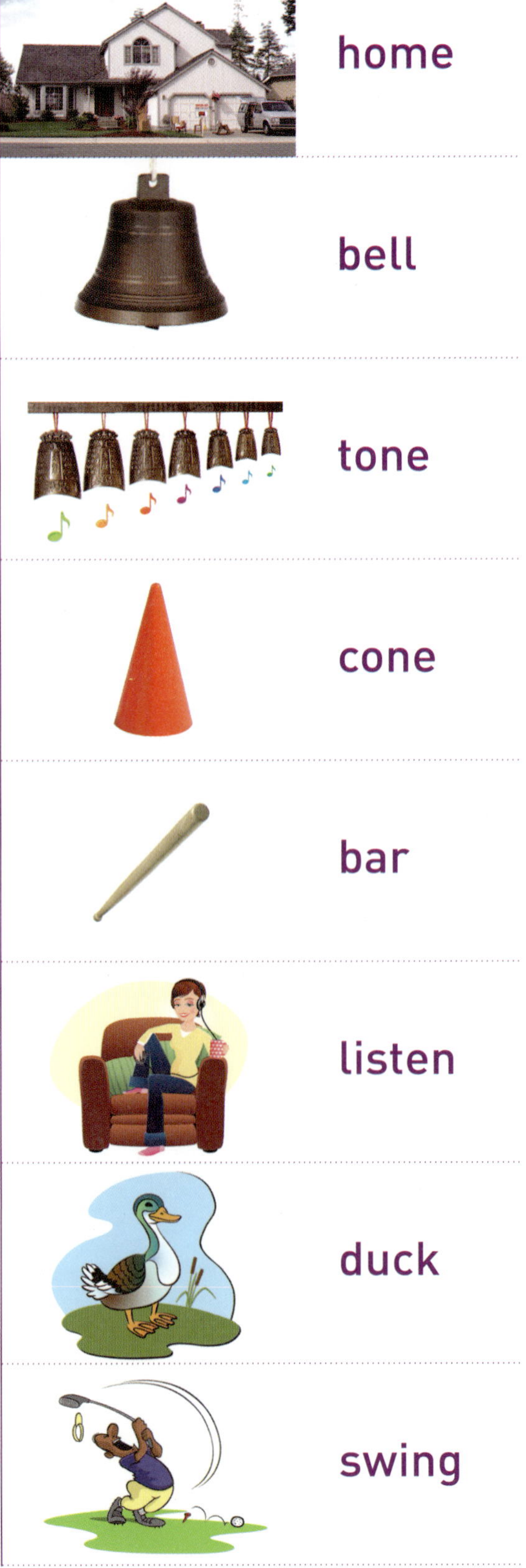

Unit 2

- home
- bell
- tone
- cone
- bar
- listen
- duck
- swing

Unit 3	rope
	rose
	hose
	nose
	pope
	clothes
	kick
	blow

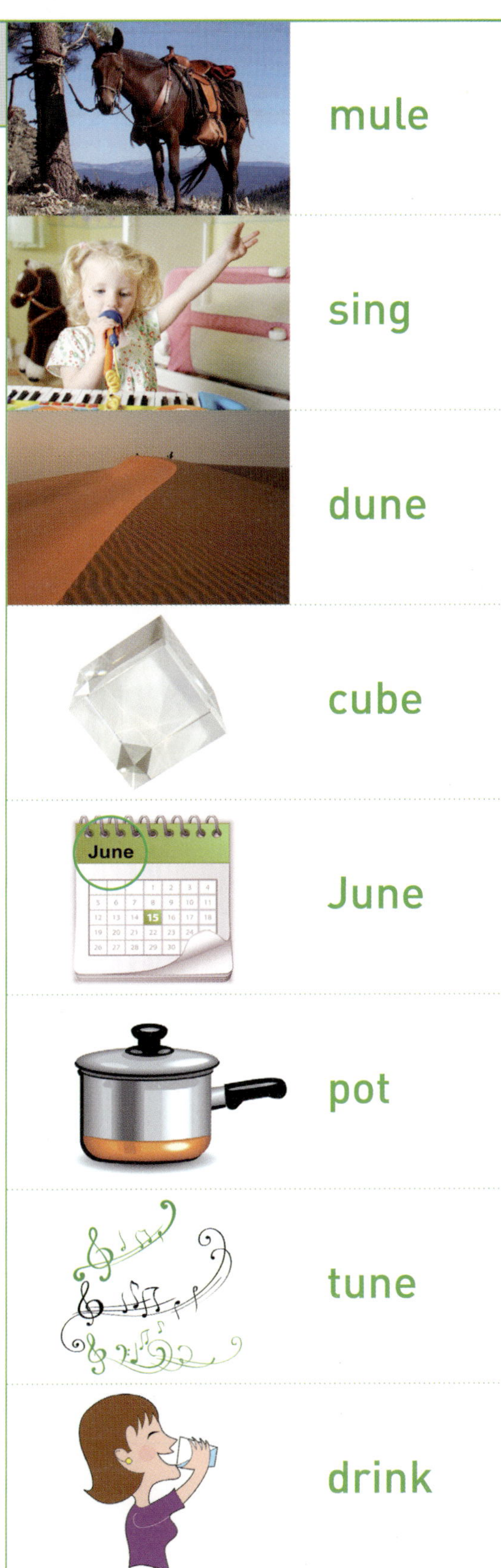

Unit 4	mule
	sing
	dune
	cube
	June
	pot
	tune
	drink

prune

melt

plum

big

walk

tune

hot

ice cube

mute

string

cute

fuse

scream

short

rope

jump

Unit
7

flute

cure

cold

sick

clock

bed

pain

smell

Unit
8

slim

class

plant

clock

eat

book

wall

tall

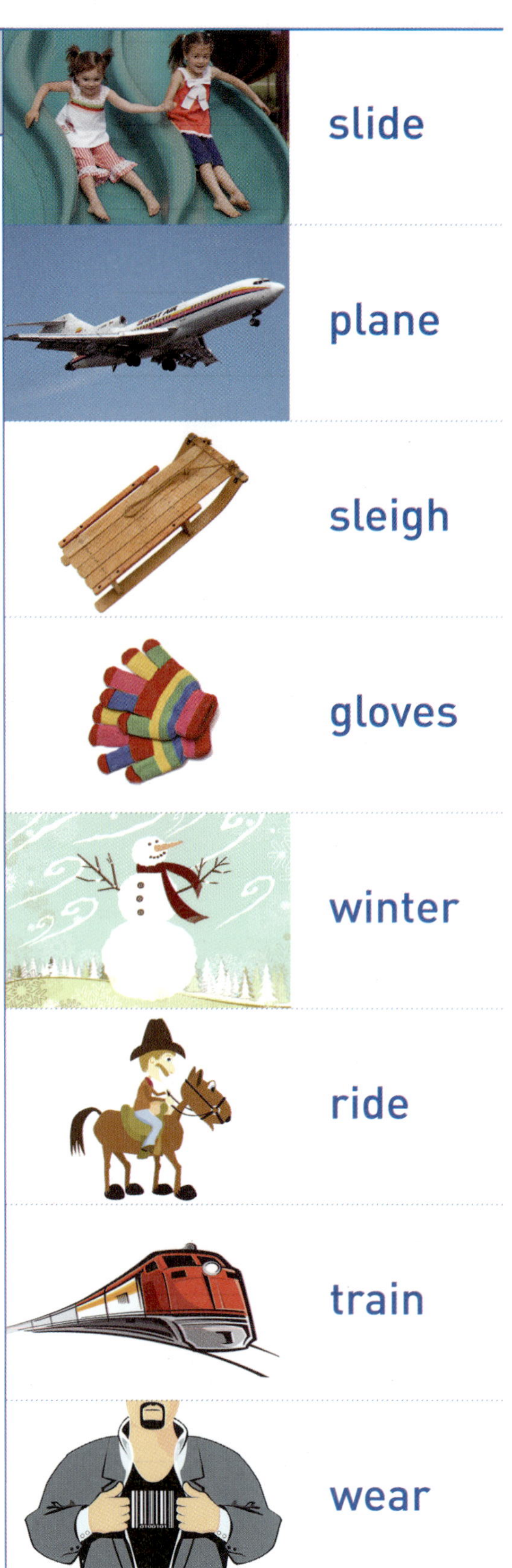

Unit 9	
	slide
	plane
	sleigh
	gloves
	winter
	ride
	train
	wear

Unit 10	
	bride
	trumpet
	drum
	frog
	groom
	piano
	wedding
	dance

drive

dress

frame

truck

lock

train

ring

gold

Memo

Gerry A. Ellim & Lawrence Herman

ISBN : 978-89-6198-193-4

Desk Copy Request / Information
To place your desk copy request or for more information,
please contact the following office:
Tel : (02) 3273-4300   Fax : (02) 3273-4303
Homepage : www.wcbooks.co.kr